12/18

D1517229

1

12 Cookies of Christmas

On the twelve days of Christmas my baker, baked for me…

Lanette Miles

12 Cookies of Christmas

On the twelve days of Christmas my baker, baked for me…

Lanette Miles
Copyright © 2018 Lanette Miles

ISBN: 9781723971563

DEDICATION
TO MY MOM.

Mary Susan Hatcher

Hello, and thank you so much for joining me for the 12 Cookies of Christmas. I wrote this book because I have a lot to share! I believe everyone has a gift. My gift is the gift of food, and in this case, baking. This is not a book that is "too this or too that". Meaning these recipes are really for everyone.

This is also not a "too fancy" recipe book that you look at the recipes and don't know what the ingredients are. It is also not same cookbook with recipes you already have.

These are tested recipes from someone who is a wife, a mom, an aunt and sister first, then a chef. I am not a home chef, I am a real chef, the professional kind. I really value recipes that work, believe me, there are so many out there that do not work, but these do and I'm sharing them with you.

My favorite holiday is Christmas. Christmas is very much about you creating memories and enriching experiences for other people around you. It's about creating traditions and passing them on so they don't get lost. Traditions are a powerful thing. If we don't do things to enrich the lives of other people, then where would we be. I am elated when the kids are excited to make cookies. We do this every year because that means there is a very good chance they will also do it with their kids, family or friends someday.

When I was a kid instead of buying presents for people we made cookies... LOTS of cookies... cookies for days! Every year we would find a new way to package them. Besides the obvious tins, we would put cookies in baskets, boxes, gift bags of all kinds, truly, whatever we could find. People loved them! We were kids that liked to play in the kitchen and make presents for people, especially when we had our Christmas break from school.

My very first memory of making cookies was actually making ornament cookies, and not the fancy kind like mine, just ornaments that we actually put on our tree. I remember my brother was very small, under 2 ,and he kept trying to eat them! My mom kept taking them away from him. I never made ornament cookies again until I was an adult.

I hope you enjoy making these cookies as much as I have enjoyed creating this book for you!

Warm Wishes and Happy Baking!

Lanette

12 Cookies of Christmas

TABLE OF CONTENTS

Eggnog Cookies

On the first day of Christmas, my baker baked for me, one dozen Eggnog Cookies!

Oh how we love eggnog at my house! It is one of my husband favorite things! There is nothing better than a soft, chewy cookie, perfectly frosted with an eggnog buttercream cookie. I am excited just thinking about it! Egg nog has so many uses in baking. I make a chocolate cake with eggnog mousse that is delectable. You can make pastry cream fill tarts with eggnog; not too mention drinking the eggnog, with our without alcohol, hot or cold. Who can forget eggnog ice-cream? Or coffee with eggnog? Obviously it has many delicious uses. When I was growing up we always made eggnog from scratch, we never bought it at the store. We made a lot of things from scratch mostly because that is how we entertained ourselves as children. We were always in the kitchen making, or baking something, usually accompanied by a huge mess! Just ask my grandmother.

I personally have never seen eggnog cookies packaged in a retail setting until I did research for this book. To be perfectly honest, we don't really buy packaged cookies at my house. I can really make you some amazing graham crackers for snacks or s'mores! With that being said, such things, do in fact exist, and they are made with… get this… REAL fresh eggs…eek! They are delightful, light and crispy!

The first time I made this particular recipe I was a Cook #1 in Maui (yes your post in a kitchen sometimes is as exciting as a number followed by a job title)! The exciting part, I actually had to literally compete with another girl for that title, so it was worth every ounce I had to give as someone who had just graduated culinary school, but had been baking all of my life. One of the most memorable times in my early days of baking was to create Christmas gifts for guest of the hotel I worked for, every day for 12 days. Of course, at a hotel your guest count can be all over the place, especially 2 weeks prior to Christmas! It was definitely a challenge, especially when your walking out the door and find out you need 17 dozen more cookies. Back to the kitchen I went! This happened often during those 12 days before Christmas.

This recipe is again so good and I have been using it for 20 years or so, and yes, there are other Eggnog Cookie recipes, but this one is really quite amazing. This is truly a crowd pleaser at any event, cookie exchange or just at home! I hope you enjoy making it!

Eggnog Cookies

Baking temperate: 400
Bake time: 10 -12 minutes
Prep time: 15 minutes
Yield: 2 dozen

INGREDIENTS

- 2 3/4 cups all-purpose flour
- 1 teaspoon nutmeg
- 1 teaspoons baking soda
- 2 teaspoons cream of tartar
- 3/4 teaspoons salt
- 1 cup butter
- 1 1/2 cups granulated white sugar
- 3 tablespoons egg nog
- 1 tablespoon bourbon
- 2 eggs

Eggnog Buttercream

- 1 pound powdered sugar sifted
- 1 1/4 cups soft unsalted butter
- 1/4 cup eggnog
- 1 tablespoon bourbon

INSTRUCTIONS

Pre heat oven to 400. In a bowl whisk together the dry cookie ingredients. In a mixer fitted with a paddle attachment, cream together butter and sugar until light and fluffy. In another bowl whisk together the eggnog, bourbon and eggs. Alternate the dry and wet ingredients. Use a small cookie scoop to scoop on a parchment lined sheet pan. Bake 10-12 minutes and let cool completely.

Next in a mixer with the paddle attachment, mix the butter, add the powdered sugar, the eggnog and bourbon. In a frosting bag fitted with your favorite tip, frost cookies. Sprinkle with fresh nutmeg.

Eggnog Buttercream

Using a star tip, start in the center and go counter clockwise, sprinkle with nutmeg.

The Perfect Sugar Cookie

On the second day of Christmas, my baker baked for me, two dozen of the Perfect Sugar Cookie.

The Perfect Sugar Cookie Recipe is NOT a roll-out cookie recipe for cookie cutters. Please see last chapter for our roll out cookies!

OK, Hopefully you have read and fully understand that this cookie does not hold a tree shape, a star or a candy cane. Do you know how many years it took us as kids to actually figure that out! So many years that we had to have been teenagers by the time we realized it was just not going to happen. We tried all kinds of things including, but not limited to, dividing, and adding more flour, substituting butter and shortening back and fourth, taking away eggs, using bread flour. Nope.. nothing, so there we were, just let the sugar cookie be a sugar cookie. We used colored sugars and egg wash. Sometimes we made colored frostings and put more sugar on top of that. Anyway you look at it, this is an amazing recipe. We chill the dough and slice it. You can also scoop and flatten it.

Ok ready for frequently asked question? What kind of sugar goes on a sugar cookie? Is that a thing I need to worry about really? Well, here is some further information to enlighten you to make your own informed decision. Truly, at one time or another, I have used all of them and there is no wrong answer, just information.

Sanding Sugar:
Sanding sugar has both large and small crystals. Sand sugar is the size of sand; slightly larger crystals than granulated. The nice thing about sanding sugar is that it holds up well under heat, so you can use it before baking or after baking as a finishing touch. Decorate your cookies before putting them in the oven, and coat them heavily to give them a solid color. You can also use sanding sugar on wet icing, just shake off the excess, and then allow the icing to dry. If you want to color your own, you can also put it in a mixer with a paddle attachment and add a few drops of color to it to make you own shades of color. If it starts to get sticky, add some cornstarch. Also sanding sugar has a bit of a natural sparkle to it that will not be affected by the heat of an oven.

Crystal Sugar:
Crystal sugar is the size of course salt, for example. It is the next stage in size and can also be known as course sugar. It is also comes in a rainbow of colors It has large crystals, which are also resistant to heat and adds extra texture and crunch to cookies. You can also color it yourself.

Granulated Sugar:
This common "table" sugar is (like all sugar) refined from sugar cane or beets; in taste tests, cane and beet sugars were indistinguishable from each other. The relatively fine crystals and neutral flavor make this sugar the most versatile sweetening agent. It can also be colored and used for cookies, the color is not as excitingly vibrant though!

The Perfect Sugar Cookie

Baking temperate: 375
Bake time: 8 minutes
Prep time: 10 minutes
Yield: 4 dozen

INGREDIENTS
• 2 1/4 cups butter
• 3 1/4 cups sugar
• 2 teaspoons vanilla
• 4 eggs
• 3/4 cup milk
• 8 cups all-purpose flour
• 2 tablespoons baking powder
• 1 teaspoon salt
• 1 tablespoon lemon zest
**** Please note, The Perfect Sugar Cookie Recipe is NOT a roll-out cookie recipe for cookie cutters. Please see last chapter for our roll out cookies!

INSTRUCTIONS
In a large mixing bowl with a paddle attachment, cream together butter, sugar and lemon zest. In a separate bowl, whisk together eggs, vanilla and milk. In another bowl, whisk together the dry ingredients. Alternating, adding in the dry and wet ingredients. Next divide cookie dough into 4 parts, roll in parchment, tie both ends. Refrigerate two hours or freeze for one hour. Remove from parchment paper, slice cookies with a knife about 1/4 inch. At this time you can bake them if your going to frost the round cookies or egg wash and sprinkle with your favorite color of sugar! Bake at 375 for 8 minutes.

Divide dough into 4 equal parts.

I like to roll the logs of dough tightly in paper

Egg wash or press your favorite colored sugar!

Chocolate Caramel Cookies

On the third day of Christmas, my baker baked for me, three dozen Chocolate Caramel Cookies.

I really love chocolate and caramel! The caramel recipe is really good for many other uses. One other suggested use is chocolate caramel tarts. It is a thick caramel that sets well. I remember the first time I made a thumbprint cookie, I did understand why you would use your thumb when there are so many other things you can use? I remember going through my grandmothers kitchen looking for a spoon or gadget to make the indentation, she had all kinds of interesting things in her kitchen. I think actually now that I remember we used my cousins thumb. It's not something that we made very often when we were kids. I never made them with my kids. It wasn't until I was working that I really saw them made all the time. I still don't use my thumb. My preferred method is actually an egg. You have to be careful not to break the egg of course, but I think it gives you the perfect size indentation.

Thumbprint cookies have been made since the 1800's, probably earlier. It's a versatile cookie that can be made with any kind of dough that you can shape into balls and press down in the center. It is said that these cookies were originally developed in Poland as a Polish Tea Cake and also referred to as a Raspberry Cave in Sweden. Almond versions were probably the earliest. Almonds were plentiful in the Middle East and Europe, so almond cookies were some of the earliest cookies. Almond paste is really easy to mold into shapes, and became widely used. This cookie was perhaps the peanut butter cup of the 19th century.

I'm not really a fan of the whole sea salt thing personally, but if you wanted to add it you could. If I were going to add it I would use smoked sea salt.

Chocolate Caramel Cookies

Baking temperate: 350
Bake time: 15 minutes
Prep time: 25 minutes
Yield: 2 dozen

INGREDIENTS
- 1 cup unsalted butter softened
- 1 cup granulated sugar
- 1 egg
- 1 tablespoon vanilla extract
- 2 cups all-purpose flour
- 1/4 cup melted chocolate
- 1/2 cup unsweetened cocoa powder
- 1 1/2 teaspoons kosher salt
- 2 tablespoons heavy cream

Caramel filling for cookies:
- 2 cups sugar
- 1/2 cup water
- 1/4 cup light corn syrup
- 1/2 cup unsalted butter
- 1/2 cup cream
- 2 tablespoons sour cream

INSTRUCTIONS
In a large bowl, using an electric mixer, cream together the butter and sugar until light and fluffy. Add the egg and vanilla. While mixer is mixing add melted chocolate, mix until incorporated. Add the flour, cocoa powder, and salt, mixing until just combined. Roll the dough into 1 inch balls and place 1 inch apart on the prepared baking sheet. Using the end of an egg or your thumb, press gently in the center of each cookie. Bake 7 minutes or until just

set. If the indentations lose their shape, gently press the centers in again. Cool on baking sheet and then transfer cookies to wire racks, and let cool completely.

 Caramel filling for cookies: cook sugar, water and corn syrup until a light caramel color, remove from heat and whisk in butter, cream and sour cream, cool completely. When your cookies are cool add caramel to them.

Scoop cookies so they are all
the same size

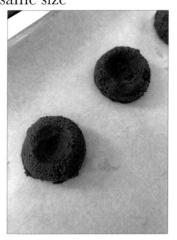

I like to use an egg to make the
indent for the caramel

Sesame Cookies

On the fourth day of Christmas, my baker baked for me, four dozen Sesame Cookies.

The first time I had a Sesame cookie, I lived on Maui and it was in early December at a luau holiday party. I remember thinking it was an excellent cookie, and since this was a cookie I wanted to add to my 12 days of Christmas gifts, then I would come up with something that was like it. I felt it would be the perfect fit to add some local Hawaiian flair. It was a huge success and I used this very recipe through many years of making cookies. It became my sons favorite Christmas cookie.

Sesame Cookies

Baking temperate: 350
Bake time:18 minutes
Prep time: 15 minutes
Yield: 5-6 dozen

INGREDIENTS
- 1 1/4 cups sesame seeds
- 2 3/4 cups all-purpose flour
- 1 teaspoon baking powder
- 1/2 teaspoon baking soda
- 1/4 tsp salt
- 1 1/2 cups butter
- 1 1/2 cups sugar
- 2 eggs
- 1 teaspoon vanilla bean paste
- 1 yolk for brushing

INSTRUCTIONS
Pre-heat oven to 350. Toast sesame seeds in hot oven on sheet pan in a single layer until golden brown, roughly 3-5 minutes stirring if needed. Cool completely. Divide sesame seeds into 3/4 cup and 1/2 cup portions. Next, in a coffee grinder or blender grind the 3/4 cup. You would like them to be coarsely ground. In a medium bowl whisk together the flour, baking powder, baking soda, salt and 3/4 cup ground sesame seeds. Next, in a bowl with a paddle attachment, cream the butter and sugar until light and fluffy. Add the eggs and dry ingredients making sure everything is well incorporated. Make dough into small discs. I like to scoop and flatten to about 1/4 inch but you can do it anyway you like. In a small bowl, wish egg yolk and 1 tablespoon of water, brush the discs with egg wash and press in sesame seeds. Place in freezer for 15 minutes or until firm. Bake 18 minutes or until golden brown.

Egg wash cookie dough

Sprinkle with sesame seeds
and freeze before baking!

Cherry White Chocolate Pistachio

On the fifth day of Christmas, my baker baked for me, five dozen Cherry White Chocolate Pistachio Cookies!

This is such a pretty cookie! It has the Christmas colors of red, green, and white. It's not super fancy, but is authentically a really great cookie and it can be baked to be soft, chewy or crunchy. This particular recipe is very versatile and you can add anything to it really. It also has won several awards through out my career and is my best selling chocolate chip cookie as well. Did you catch that? I'm sharing the best selling, award winning chocolate chip cookie recipe with you! I do love cookies. In fact, they are one of my favorite things. This is a very easy recipe and is quite straight forward. I remember having to make scoop cookies for 8 hours straight. I never stopped loving the cookies but my wrist did start to hurt. I worked in a hotel in Phoenix and I always avoided the cookie scooping projects after that. We sold a lot of cookies at that hotel as well, it's because they were so good. I was glad we made the cookies from scratch.

I had worked in a casino bakery and they used frozen cookie dough. Being slightly naive, I didn't know you could buy pre-packaged frozen dough. Even though very early on in my career, I honestly don't ever remember hearing about frozen cookie dough in boxes at culinary school either. Why would they buy cookies dough if they had a bakery department? They had staff who could bake, all of the equipment and ingredients to do it. I did my own cost investigating and brought my recipes to the chef, and with all my charm, convinced him that we could do much better. (Oh goodness me and my great ideas) So again, back to making cookies, I still did avoid the scooping part this time. People raved about the improvement of our cookies. I hope you add this cookie to one of your favorites.

Cherry White Chocolate Pistachio

Baking temperate: 350
Bake time: 12-14 minutes
Prep time:10 minutes
Yield: 3 dozen

INGREDIENTS

- 1 1/2 cups unsalted butter
- 1 1/4 cup brown sugar
- 1 1/8 cup white sugar
- 3 eggs
- 1 tablespoon vanilla
- 3 3/4 cups all-purpose flour
- 1/2 teaspoon salt
- 3/4 teaspoon baking soda
- 3/4 teaspoon baking powder
- 1 cup white chocolate chips
- 3/4 cup pistachios
- 3/4 cup dried cherries

INSTRUCTIONS

Cream the sugars and butter very well until light and fluffy. The color will become lighter as you are mixing air into it. Add eggs, one at a time, mix thoroughly. In a separate bowl, measure dry ingredients and add gradually. Next, add the vanilla, chocolate chips, nuts and cherries. Scoop on a sheet pan or cookie sheet lined with parchment paper and flatten. Bake 12-14 minutes. Cookies can be baked to be soft at 12 minutes or crispy at14 minutes.

I use the blue scoop for this cookie. It is what I consider a large cookie but not a jumbo.

Christmas Fruit Cookie

On the sixth day of Christmas, my baker baked for me, six dozen Christmas Fruit Cookies!

This is a really good cookie. I know most people frown upon Christmas fruit, but if you make it yourself from scratch, its actually quite amazing. It is well balanced, not too sugary or sweet at all. I have never used the Christmas fruit from the store on this cookie ever. But I have tasted other peoples Christmas fruit cookies and this tastes nothing like that at all. So you are safe! People also use dried fruit in cookies and scones all the time.

Christmas Fruit Cookie

Baking temperate: 350
Bake time: 16-18 minutes
Prep time: 24 hours and 15 minutes
Yield: 2 dozen

INGREDIENTS

- 2 cups all-purpose flour
- 1/2 teaspoon salt
- 1 teaspoon baking soda
- 1 teaspoon baking powder
- 1 tablespoon vanilla
- 3 tablespoons fruit liquid
- 2 eggs
- 1 cup unsalted butter - room temperature
- 1 cup dark brown sugar
- 1/2 cup granulated sugar
- 3 cups old fashioned oats
- 1 1/2 cups Christmas Fruit
- 1 cup dark rum
- 1 cup apple brandy
- 1/4 cup Grand Marnier
- 1/2 teaspoon fresh nutmeg
- 2 cinnamon sticks
- 1/2 tablespoon orange and lemon zest
- (Please note you can use any kind of dried fruit for this)
- 1/4 cup dried apple chopped
- 1/4 cup dried pineapple chopped
- 1/4 cup dried currents
- 1/4 cup dried mango chopped
- 1/4 cup dried apricots chopped
- 1/4 cup dried golden raisins chopped

INSTRUCTIONS

First, you will need to make the Christmas fruit listed in the last recipe. If you have a few days to let it set, that is preferred, otherwise, 24 hours will be fine. You will need to take all of the ingredients for the Christmas fruit and place them in a pot, bring to a full boil, remove from heat. Let cool at room temperature. Once completely cool; refrigerate overnight. When you are ready to make your cookies, take out the cinnamon sticks and strain any excess liquid that has not reconstituted the fruit. Set this liquid aside, you will need it for the cookies. If you have more than you need you can always add it to some spiced cider.

In a medium bowl, mix together the flour, salt, baking soda and baking powder. In another bowl, whisk together the eggs, vanilla, and the fruit liquid. In a mixer with the paddle attachment, cream the butter and sugar's together until light and fluffy, alternating the eggs and flour. Next add the oats until just mixed together, remove from mixer. Gently fold in Christmas fruit, making sure its incorporated well. Scoop cookie dough and flatten. Refrigerate 2 hours or until firm. Next place on parchment lined baking sheets about 3 inches apart. Bake at 350 for 16-18 minutes. Turn half way through. The cookies will be golden but still slightly soft in the middle. Let cool on baking sheets.

Clementine Meringue Cookies

On the seventh day of Christmas, my baker baked for me, seven dozen
Clementine Meringue Cookies!

This is a cookie that is crunchy and chewy with a beautiful clementine orange filling. It is not a typical crunchy meringue cookie. Meringue is light,
airy, and sweet. They are crisp on the outside and soft on the inside. They
seem as if they will melt in your mouth. In order to achieve that texture
meringue cookies require, preparations such as, beating ingredients until
light and fluffy, and cooking for a longer time under a lower temperature until meringue becomes dry on the outside is pertinent.

The term, Meringue, actually first appeared in a French cookbook written by François Massialot in 1692, interestingly there was an earlier recorded English manuscript book in 1604 by Lady Elinor Fettiplace, who gave a recipe that can be easily recognizable as a Swiss meringue. She called this recipe "white biskit bread." This explains why Sweetooth credited this cookie to UK as the place of origin while Lady Elinor Fettiplace lived in Berkshire.

A child today would probably be disappointed by the goodies found in the Christmas stockings of the past. Not a single electronic or game, but instead, the likes of candies, nuts, and fresh clementine oranges, all of which were considered to be a real treat at the time. For some families, especially ones that lived in cold areas, oranges were an exotic treat. Giving the orange is a way to celebrate generosity and caring for others without thinking about a gift in return. This tradition dates back to Salt Nicholas along with nuts children would get fresh oranges for Christmas.

We have always gotten oranges in our stockings. Santa has continues the tradition with my kids as well. He also gives them chocolate oranges every year. I believe creating memories and traditions is so important for our kids!
Thank you Santa!

Meringue Tips:
Clean whisk and bowl, leaving no traces of oil, butter, or spray of any kind. If your eggs are not whipping up quickly, a tainted bowl could be the reason.

A great way to bring your eggs up to room temperature quickly, is to put them in a bowl of hot water for two minutes. Then proceed to crack eggs and continue.

Clementine Meringue Cookies

Baking temperate: 225
Bake time: 60 minutes+
Prep time: 20 minutes
Yield: 18

INGREDIENTS
- 4 egg whites room temperate
- Pinch of salt
- 1 cup sugar
- 1 1/2 teaspoon cornstarch sifted
- 1 teaspoon lemon juice
- 1 teaspoon vanilla bean paste
-

  Clementine Filling
- 4 egg yolks
- 1 whole egg
- 1 cup sugar
- 1/2 cup fresh clementine juice
- 1/2 cup unsalted butter
- 1 tablespoon clementine zest

INSTRUCTIONS
In a mixer bowl fitted with a whisk attachment, whisk egg whites on high speed until foamy, add salt. Soft peaks will start to form. Reduce speed to medium and while mixer is running, add sugar, slowly. Once done, add sugar, increase speed to high and continue whisking until stiff peaks form, meringue is glossy, and the sugar is fully dissolved. Add cornstarch, lemon, and vanilla bean then whisk on low speed just until combined. Line baking

sheet with parchment paper. You can pipe cookies with a pastry tip. I like a more fluffy pillow look so I scoop them, then with the back on a spoon fluff them. I leave a small indent in the top for the clementine to go. Bake on bottom rack of oven for 60 minutes. Turn the oven off and let them cool in the oven. Do not be alarmed if they crack. Next make the clementine filling. In a bowl, whisk together all of the ingredients except the butter and the zest. Transfer the whisked ingredients into a heavy bottom pot, cook on low, stirring with a wooden spoon or plastic spatula until it coats the back of the spoon. You will need a fine mesh strainer. Next strain the hot mixture into a mixing bowl fitted with the whisk attachment. Mix on medium speed. This will both help incorporate the butter and cool the mixture. Add the butter 1 piece at a time and add the zest. Remove from the mixer and transfer to a glass or plastic bowl. Cover with plastic wrap on the surface, cool completely. Final step is to add the clementine to the cookies! You can also garnish with sectioned clementine if you wish!

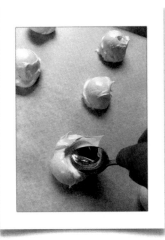

Indent

Scoop

Bake

Peppermint Candy Cane Cookies

On the eighth day of Christmas, my baker baked for me, eight dozen Peppermint Candy Cane Cookies.

A choirmaster, in 1670, was worried about the children sitting quietly all through the long Christmas nativity service. So he asked a local candy maker to make them something to eat to keep them quiet! As he wanted to remind them of Christmas, he made them into a 'J' shape like a shepherds crook, to remind them of the shepherds that visited the baby Jesus at the first Christmas. Sometime around 1900 the red stripes were added and they were flavored with peppermint or wintergreen. From Germany, candy canes spread to other parts of Europe, where they were handed out during plays reenacting the Nativity. As such, according to this legend, the candy cane became associated with Christmastide.

The earliest verifiable reference to stick candy is a record of the 1837 Exhibition of the Massachusetts Charitable Mechanic Association, where confections were judged competitively. A recipe for straight peppermint candy sticks, white with red stripes, was published in 1844. The "candy cane" is found in literature in 1866, Its earliest known association with Christmas was in 1874, and by 1882, canes were being hung on Christmas trees. As with other forms of stick candy, the earliest canes were manufactured by hand. Chicago confectioners, the Bunte Brothers, filed one of the earliest patents for candy cane making machines in the early 1920's.

I do remember making this cookie during Christmas break! Do you? Did you ever make this cookie? I know it is very popular and there are a lot of recipes for this cookie. I like to use powdered red color, but gel color will work also. However, if you use the liquid color your red might turn pink. You can also add green if you would like. I like chocolate and peppermint together so I have also done that combination. You can just divide the dough in half and color it accordingly.

Peppermint Candy Cane Cookies

Baking temperate: 375
Bake time: 8 minutes
Prep time: 25+
Yield: 2 dozen

INGREDIENTS
- 2 cups unsalted butter room temp
- 1 tablespoon vanilla bean paste
- 1 tablespoon peppermint extract
- 1 1/2 cups powdered sugar
- 3 3/4 cups bread flour
- 1/4 cup dark cocoa powder
- 1/4 teaspoon salt

INSTRUCTIONS
In a mixer with paddle attachment, cream butter and sugar until light and fluffy. Then add the peppermint and vanilla bean. Next with the mixer on low, add the bread flour. Remove from mixer and divide into 4 equal parts. Place one of the divided pieces back in the mixer and add the cocoa powder. Remove from mixer and with another piece of dough, mix in the red gel color until its dark red. Wrap the 4 doughs in plastic and refrigerate one hour. Next you will divide each dough into 4 pieces and roll them like a snake, all the exact same size. (about 1/2 inch round pieces 4 inches long). This does not have to be exact. If you like them thinner or thicker you can do either one. Next you will pick two colors, feel free to mix and match. You will then twist the dough and make the crook in the neck. Place on cookie sheets and freeze 30 minutes. Then bake 8-10 minutes.

Candy Canes ready for the oven!

Roll and twist dough.

Snowflakes of Gingerbread

On the ninth day of Christmas my baker baked for me, nine dozen
Snowflakes of Gingerbread Cookies!

I have a lot of experience with gingerbread! So fun! When I was working at
the Sheraton in Seattle, I built Venice out of gingerbread. That was one of
the first times I had collaborated with others on such a project. An Architect
firm and I spent 140 hours on this project. It was later sold at an auction for
$125,000.00. The money, and the gingerbread house, were donated to the
Seattle Children's Hospital. What a great reason to bake!

There is a big difference in the structure of gingerbread cookies and gingerbread for building houses.

Nothing screams holidays quite like gingerbread in its many forms; edible houses, gingerbread men, to spiced loaves. In Medieval England, the term gingerbread simply meant "preserved ginger" and wasn't applied to the desserts we are familiar with until the 15th century. Ginger root was first cultivated in ancient China, where it was commonly used as a medical treatment. From there it spread to Europe via the Silk Road.

The first known recipe for gingerbread came from Greece in 2400 B.C. Chinese recipes were developed during the 10th century and by the late Middle Ages, Europeans had their own version of gingerbread. The hard cookies, sometimes gilded with gold leaf and shaped like animals, kings and queens, were a staple at Medieval fairs in England, France, Holland and Germany. Queen Elizabeth I is credited with the idea of decorating the cookies in this fashion, after she had some made to resemble the dignitaries visiting her court.

Over time some of these festivals came to be known as Gingerbread Fairs, and the gingerbread cookies served there were known as "fairings". The shapes of the gingerbread changed with the season, including flowers in the spring and birds in the fall. Elaborately decorated gingerbread became synonymous with all things fancy and elegant in England. The gold leaf that was often used to decorate gingerbread cookies led to the popular expression "to take the gilt off of gingerbread".

Gingerbread houses originated in Germany during the 16th century. The elaborate cookie-walled houses, decorated with foil in addition to gold leaf, became associated with Christmas tradition. Their popularity rose when the Brothers Grimm wrote the story of Hansel and Gretel, in which the main characters stumble upon a house made entirely of treats deep in the forest. It is unclear whether or not gingerbread houses were a result of the popular fairy tale, or vice versa. Gingerbread wasn't available to the masses, though. European royalty permitted it to be prepared only by a specially trained gingerbread guild, and common folk could enjoy the sweet dessert only during the Christmas.

Snowflakes of Gingerbread

Baking temperate: 350
Bake time: 8-10 minutes
Prep time:15+chill time
Yield: 24

INGREDIENTS

- 6 cups all-purpose flour plus more for surface
- 1 teaspoon baking soda
- 1/2 teaspoon baking powder
- 1 cup unsalted butter
- 1 cup dark brown sugar
- 1 tablespoon ground ginger
- 1 tablespoon ground cinnamon
- 1 1/2 teaspoons ground cloves
- 1 1/2 teaspoons ground nutmeg
- 2 eggs
- 1 tablespoon vanilla
- 1 cup un-sulfured molasses

Decorating options:

Powdered sugar dusting, white chocolate, royal icing (see last chapter for recipe) We use sprinkles, sugars and dragees.

INSTRUCTIONS:

Sift together all dry ingredients. In a mixing bowl fitted with a paddle attachment, cream butter and sugar until light and fluffy. Next add eggs one at a time, followed by vanilla and molasses. Carefully add the dry ingredients while the mixer in going. Divide dough in half and flatten. Wrap in plastic wrap and refrigerate one hour. Let dough sit at room temp 15 minutes. On a well dusted surface, roll out your dough to 1/4 inch thick. Use your snowflake cutter to cut unto desired shapes. Refrigerate until very firm or freeze 15 minutes. Bake at 350 for 8-10 minutes.

Cookies rolled and ready for the oven.

Powdered sugar for a simple look.

In the second version of this cookie I use melted white chocolate and gold dragees.

We use edible metallic paint and a sponge to make this antique look. You can buy the paint at your local cake store, online or very easily mix your own by adding a couple drops of 80 proof or higher alcohol to your favorite color of luster dust, petal dust or powdered color. The alcohol will evaporate and you can also use brushes to paint as well.

Chocolate Chestnut Cookies

On the tenth day of Christmas, my baker baked for me, ten dozen Chocolate Chestnut Cookies.

Im sure you have all heard the song about chestnuts roasting on an open fire. I'm pretty sure nothing says old fashioned Christmas more than chestnuts. I have explained the process of how to roast and shell them below. However you can also buy them already shelled and in a paste form at some grocery stores or online. I like the idea of the roasting process and I don't mind doing it at all, so that is why I have explained it for you. This is a really great sandwich cookie recipe. You can also substitute filling for different flavors.

Chocolate Chestnut Cookies

Baking temperate: 350
Bake time: 8-10 minutes
Prep time: 1 hour
Yield: 2-3 dozen

INGREDIENTS
- 5 oz. chestnuts + more for filling see below
- 2 tablespoons brown sugar
- 2 1/4 cups all-purpose flour
- 1/4 tsp baking powder
- 1/4 tsp salt
- 1 cup unsalted butter
- 1/2 cup powdered sugar
- 1 egg
- 1 tablespoon vanilla

Filling
- 20 chestnuts peeled and roasted (see below)
- 1/2 cup milk
- 1/2 cup sugar
- 1/2 cup water
- 1 tablespoon vanilla bean paste
- 2 tablespoons brandy
- 1/2 cup chocolate chips
- 1/2 cup cream

INSTRUCTIONS
Please see on next page for toasting chestnuts. You will need 5 oz. for the cookie portion. Place roasted chestnuts and light brown sugar in a food processor, or blender and pulse until nuts are finely ground. Whisk together chestnuts, all-purpose flour, baking powder, and salt in a small bowl. Using a

paddle attachment in a stand mixer, mix together softened butter and powdered sugar at medium-high speed until light and fluffy. Reduce mixer speed to low and gradually add the chestnut mixture until just combined. Beat in the egg and vanilla extract until dough comes together. Divide into two equal disks, cover with plastic wrap and refrigerate for at least 1 hour. Roll out onto floured surface then cut. Make sure you end up with an even number (top and bottom). Freeze for 15 minutes before baking. Bake cookies until golden, about 10-12 minutes.

Chestnuts

Preheat your oven to 425. Make a large X slice across the rounded top of the chestnuts with a sharp serrated bread knife. Be sure to cut through the shell only.

Place cut chestnuts in a small saucepan and cover with water. Bring to a slow boil. Remove the chestnuts from the water and place them on a parchment lined baking sheet. Roast 25 minutes, or until the shells begin to open where you cut into them. Take out of oven. Put in a bowl and cover with a towel for 15 minutes to allow them to steam. Then proceed to peeling them. **Take your 5oz. for cookies at this step.**

In a medium saucepan over medium-high heat, simmer chestnuts with milk until soft, 12 minutes. Make the simple syrup by combining the sugar and water in a small saucepan and bring to a boil until the sugar dissolves. Drain chestnuts and puree in a food processor with the simple syrup until smooth. Transfer to a medium bowl and chill in the refrigerator until cool. Next boil the cream and whisk in chocolate chips to make ganache. Cool at room temperature. Next whisk together ganache and chestnut for filling. Carefully fill each cookie.

Chestnuts!

Chestnut Dough is very easy to work with and rolls out nicely.

You can use any kind of cookie cutters for this. Just make sure you have enough for the top and bottoms!

Turn over the bottoms of the cookies flat side up. That is where you will put the filling.

Powdered sugar the tops.

48

Nutcracker Biscotti

On the eleventh day of Christmas, my baker baked for me, 11 dozen Nutcracker Biscotti.

I remember when I was I kid my grandparents had a wood stove and my grandpa would put nuts in the shell on top of the fire and then crack them with an old fashioned nut cracker. The nutcracker was not the hand held kind. It was a Get Crackin' brand nutcracker. He had several nut trees around his property. We always had nuts in our Christmas stockings. As I got older, I thought this little thing was such an important part of our holiday. My grandpa made sure there were nuts in our Christmas stockings, it was so important to him. I'm not sure if we ever actually ate all of them. I know they went in some sling shots one year. At least a few times over the years, the boys would get yelled at for throwing them at each other!

St. Nicholas of Myra is a major saint in many European and Eastern countries, and one of the old Christian traditions surrounding his feast day is for kids to leave their shoes out overnight in front of the fireplace, or outside their bedroom door so that St. Nicholas can fill them with nuts.

Nuts were historically opened using a hammer and anvil, During the Victorian era, fruit and nuts were presented at dinner. Ornate and often silver-plated nutcrackers were produced to accompany them on the dinner table. Nuts have long been a popular choice for desserts, throughout Europe. The nutcrackers were placed on dining tables to serve as a fun and entertaining center of conversation while diners awaited their final course.

The spring-jointed nutcracker was patented in 1913, and a design similar to a car jack, that gradually increases pressure on the shell to avoid damaging the kernel inside is used by the Crackerjack company, patented in 1947. Figurative nutcrackers are a good luck symbol in Germany, and a folk tale recounts that a puppet-maker won a nut cracking challenge by creating a doll with a mouth for a lever to crack the nuts.

The origin of the Nutcracker Ballet, a classic Christmas Story, is a fairy tale ballet in two acts centered on a family's Christmas Eve celebration. The play commissioned by the director of Moscow's Imperial in 1891, and premiered a week before Christmas 1892. Since premiering in western countries in the 1940's, this ballet has become perhaps the most popular to be performed around Christmas time.

Decorative nutcrackers became popular in the US after World War II, following the first US production of *The Nutcracker* ballet in 1940 and the exposure of US soldiers to the dolls during the war. In the United States, few of the decorative nutcrackers are now functional, though expensive working designs are still available.

Nutcracker Biscotti

Baking temperate: 325
Bake time: 28+18
Prep time: 15 minutes
Yield: 1 dozen

INGREDIENTS
2 1/4 cups flour
1 1/2 teaspoons baking powder
3/4 teaspoons salt
6 tablespoons unsalted butter
3/4 cup sugar
2 eggs
1 tablespoon vanilla
1 teaspoon lemon zest
1/2 cup almonds
1/2 cup hazelnuts
1/4 cup pistachios
1/4 cup pecans
1/4 cup cashews
Chocolate white or dark (optional) for drizzling or dipping

INSTRUCTIONS
Sift dry ingredients, cream butter and sugar, add eggs in one at a time. Mix in vanilla and lemon. Next add the flour, being careful not to over mix. I prefer the nuts are similar in size, so if you feel you may need to dice them, feel free; you can also substitute the nuts for any kind. Mix the nuts in by hand. Dough will be sticky. Place dough on a well floured surface, roll into a 15 inch log. Flatten the top slightly. Bake until firm, roughly 28 minutes. Cool completely, slice 1 inch thick, bake 9 minutes on each side. You can dip them in chocolate, stripe them in chocolate or just have plain.

Roll into a log and flatten top.

First bake!

Second bake, 9 minutes on each side.

Slice when completely cool.

Christmas Ornament Cookies

On the twelfth day of Christmas, my baker baked for me, twelve dozen Christmas Ornament Cookies, and it was enough to decorate my whole tree!

This in not your run of the mill sugar cookie cut out recipe. It has a very different flavor and is not overly sweet. It has nice balance and is easy to work with. The cookies you make can be any shape. They do not have to be ornaments. Also they can be rolled out to your desired thickness. Cookies can be put in cellophane bags and given as gift. Just make sure your decorated cookies are dry before packaging. I personally use this recipe for any cookie that has to be decorated because it does have durability and tastes good. As far as decorating goes I use fondant, buttercream, and royal icing. All of those recipes are also in the next few pages. You can use all kinds of different decorating techniques. I like using fondant and stencils. You can also pipe them or use royal icing and stencils with butter cream. Or can also just free hand your design! I also use sugars, sprinkles and dragees in gold, silver and multicolors. Gel colors are my preference because they hold the color. You can purchase a lot of these things on my blogs shopping page as well. I have found that it can be a bit of a challenge getting some supplies for decorating if you don't live in a city that has an authentic cake decorating store. There are big brand craft stores. I use purchased fondant already colored but you are more than welcome to either color white fondant or make your own fondant. I personally never got into making my own, but if you do, it is quite good, just a little time consuming in my opinion. As far as the stencils, you can use all kinds of stencils. I would venture off to your craft or hardware store to see what you can find, and of course you can also find them online.

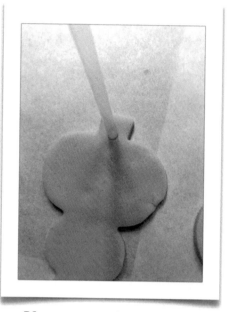

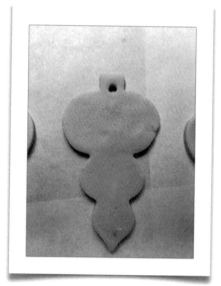

If you are going to hang your ornaments make sure you poke holes in them before you bake them and make sure your cookies are a little thicker. Also make sure that you poke the hole right after you place the fondant on the cookie.

You are going to roll out the fondant to about 1/4 inch thickness, lift off paper, put back on paper, place stencil on top of fondant and roll over the top of the fondant. You will see the fondant has risen from the stencil and you will then spray lightly wait for about one minute. At the minute mark, the spray will still be wet.

Christmas Ornament Cookies

Baking temperate: 325
Bake time: 15-18 minutes
Prep time: 10+decorating
Yield: 12-16 depending on your cutters

INGREDIENTS

- 2 cups unsalted butter cold
- 1 cup brown sugar
- 1 tablespoon vanilla
- 1 teaspoon salt
- 1 lb. 2 oz. bread flour
- 1/2 cup cornstarch

INSTRUCTIONS

Mix all ingredients together until they clump together. Make sure the butter is fully incorporated. Shape in a disc, wrap in plastic wrap and refrigerate. Let sit at room temp for 30 minutes. Roll out cookies on floured surface or on parchment. As for the thickness of these cookies, it depends on your application. We use this recipe for all of our decorated cookies. The ornaments we usually do 1/4 inch thick. Punch a hole in your cookies if you are going to put a ribbon on the top (optional). You would need to do this before you bake them, I use a straw to cut out a small circle, making sure its centered so its strong enough to hold the cookies. Freeze cookies 20 minutes before baking, bake at 325. They will be slightly brown around the edges, cool completely.

Your Ideas!

Carefully remove the stencil and using the same cutter that you used for the dough to cut out the fondant.

Frost the back of the cookie for flat surface, carefully, add the fondant cutout to the cookie. If you are hanging the ornaments you should put the hole in the fondant at this time.

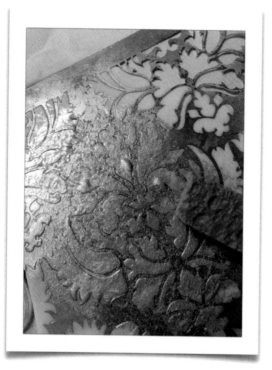

We are using a very beautiful damask stencil, with edible silver paint, and a sponge to make this antique look. You can buy the paint at your local cake store, online, or very easily mix your own by adding a couple drops of 80 proof or higher alcohol to your favorite color of luster dust, petal dust or powdered color.

The alcohol will evaporate and you can also use brushes to paint as well. Also you want to pull the stencil away from you, not towards you when you remove it. Remember it will be wet.

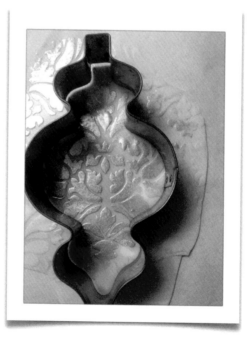

Royal Icing

- 3 egg whites, at room temperature
- 4 1/2 cups powdered sugar
- 1/2 tsp. cream of tartar
- Pinch of salt
- 1 teaspoon vanilla
- 1 teaspoon lemon juice

In the bowl, use an electric mixer fitted with the whisk attachment, beat the egg whites, powdered sugar, cream of tartar and salt on medium-low speed until blended. Add the vanilla or lemon juice, increase the speed to medium-high, and continue beating until stiff peaks form and the mixture nearly triples in volume (approximately 7 to 8 minutes). As your working with this icing keep covered with a wet paper towel.

Royal Icing

- 4 cups powdered sugar
- 3 tablespoons meringue powder
- 6-8 tablespoons of warm water
- 1 teaspoon vanilla
- 1 teaspoon lemon juice

In the bowl, with an electric mixer fitted with a whisk attachment, beat all of the ingredients together 7-8 minutes. Icing will keep in airtight container. As your working with this icing, keep covered with a wet paper towel.

The Cake Contessa's Buttercream

2 lbs. powdered sugar
1 pound unsalted butter
8 oz. shortening
1 tablespoon lemon
2 tablespoons vanilla or 1 tablespoon vanilla bean paste
1 tablespoon meringue powder

Mix all together in a stand mixer until well combined.

Eggnog

Did you know the George Washington served eggnog during the Holidays? In Britain, the drink was originally popular among the aristocrats. Milk, eggs, and sherry were foods of the wealthy, so eggnog was often used in toasts to prosperity and good health at royal events during the holiday season. In the United States Eggnog was mixed with all kinds of alcohol even moonshine when bourbon and brandy were too expensive. Traditional eggnog has a significant fat content, due to the use of cream, and a high sugar content. Ingredients vary significantly between different recipes. Alcohol used in different national and regional versions of eggnog. I hope you enjoy this recipe.

Eggnog

Cook time: 20 minutes
Prep time: 5 minutes
Yield: 1 quart (4 to 5 cups more if you add alcohol)

INGREDIENTS
- 6 egg yolks
- 3/4 cup sugar
- 2 cups whole milk
- 2 whole cloves
- 1/2 teaspoon cinnamon
- 1 cup heavy cream
- 1 teaspoon freshly grated nutmeg
- 1 1/2 teaspoons vanilla extract
-

INSTRUCTIONS
In a large bowl, use a whisk to mix egg yolks until they become somewhat light in color. Slowly add the sugar, beating after each addition. Beat at high speed or whisk until fluffy. Heat milk with cinnamon and cloves. Combine the milk, cloves, and cinnamon in a heavy-bottomed saucepan. Slowly heat on medium heat until the milk mixture is hot, but not boiling. Temper the eggs by slowly adding half of the hot milk mixture into the eggs, whisking constantly while you add the hot mixture. Pour the mixture back into the saucepan.

Cook until eggnog mixture thickens. Cook the eggnog on medium heat, stirring constantly with a wooden spoon, until the mixture begins to thicken slightly, and coats the back of the spoon. It helps to have a candy thermometer, but not necessary; if you have one, cook until the mixture reaches 160°F. Remove from heat and stir in the cream. Strain, add vanilla and nutmeg. Then chill. At this point you can add rum, brandy or bourbon.

Hot Chocolate

Hot Chocolate was introduced to Europe by Mexico. It started by being a very strong taste because the cultivation of sugar was not in existence yet. The original drink was vastly consumed by natives and people all over Mexico and Central America because that is where is grew.

Cortez had taken cocoa beans and chocolate drink making equipment with them back to Spain. The Royal Spanish Family considered hot chocolate to be very fashionable. Later, sugar was introduced to the recipe however it was still very expensive in Europe because at that time the cocoa was not grown in Europe. The first cocoa powder producing machine was invented in the Netherlands in 1828. I think it's fun that they used to have chocolate houses in Europe like we have coffee houses.

Hot chocolate was first brought to North America as early as the 17th century by the Dutch. The first time colonists began selling hot chocolate was around 1755. We love hot chocolate and all of its amazing varieties!

Hot Chocolate

Yield: 6-8 cups

INGREDIENTS

1 cup chocolate chips
1 cup heavy cream
1/4 cup sugar optional
4 cups whole milk
whip cream optional

INSTRUCTIONS

In a heavy bottom saucepan, boil cream, whisk in chocolate chips, add the milk and sugar. Heat completely, carefully pour into your favorite mugs.

Spiced Cider

Spiced Cider is often associated with Yuletide! People used to gather to actually bless the next apple harvest season by celebrating with this Yuletide drink. This event took place on the twelfth night of the Christmas Season! When the Romans arrived in the British Isles around 55 B.C. the English were drinking cider! The Orchards that Jonny Appleseed planted across the U.S. were originally intended for cider suppliers, not pie bakers. This recipe does not contain alcohol but you can add it if you like wine, brandy, bourbon or tequila. All compliment this drink well. Spiced cider is a drink you can find all over the world in different variations.

Spiced Cider

Cook time: 15
Prep time: 5
Yield: 1 gallon (16 cups)

INGREDIENTS

- 1 gallon apple juice or apple cider
- 1 orange sliced
- 4 cinnamon sticks
- 4 cloves
- 1 teaspoon allspice
- 1 teaspoon nutmeg
- 1/2 cup brown sugar

INSTRUCTIONS
Boil all ingredients together in a heavy bottom saucepan. Ladle into cups and enjoy.

RESOURCES

HERE IS THE LINK TO MY BLOG WHERE YOU CAN FIND SPRINKLES, SPARKLES, COOKIE CUTTERS, COLORED FONDANT AND MORE!

WWW.CONTESSACATERINGTHEBLOG.COM

NOTES

YOU CAN USE THIS SPACE FOR YOUR OWN NOTES. I REALLY HOPE YOU ENJOYED MAKING COOKIES!

ABOUT THE AUTHOR

Hi! I'm Lanette, I live in a very tiny town in Washington State. However, I travel for events all over the world. I am married. I love, love, love my husband Travis very much. We have 3 kids, Bryson, Oztin, and Kimo. We also have a new granddaughter!

Our newest adventure is a food blog, which I am over the moon excited about! I love to teach people things; little tricks that I have picked up along the way. I also love to share my gadgets that I know work and recipes that I have used in many kitchens around the globe. I'm excited also to share with you many inspirations that are part of what I love about what I do. The prettiness of the events, the ruffles, the candles and sparkles all never cease to make my eyes twinkle
and my heart warm.

I am also a great resource, so if you have questions that are food or event related, please ask and I will do my best to get back to you!

Contessa's is our catering division and has been in the food and beverage industry for 22 years, working at several upscale resorts such as the Royal Hawaiian in Oahu, Kapalua Bay hotel in Maui, Ritz Carlton in Phoenix, and numerous in Mexico. In all of these resorts, our chefs have worked side by side with some of the best chefs in the country. I graduated from the Art Institute of Seattle with a full degree in Food Science. I have been on several food expeditions throughout Mexico and many regions of the U.S.

These are my gifts to share. It is my belief that each person in this world has a gift. Amazing food and beautiful events are mine. It is my passion. I create memorable experiences for truly wonderful people. Please let me share my gifts with you!

36172060R00040

Made in the USA
Columbia, SC
24 November 2018